Command Your Destiny

Take Control of Your Life

Command Your Destiny

Take Control of Your Life

EDGAR L. VANN

EDGAR VANN MINISTRIES
14601 Dequindre, Detroit, Michigan 48212

For more information, call (313) 867-4700.

Reach us on the Internet:

www.edgarvannministries.com.

ISBN 978-0-9847217-0-2

For Worldwide Distribution.

Printed in the U.S.A.

Acknowledgements

Words are inadequate to express my love and gratitude for those without whom this book would not be possible.

My wife, Sheila, my partner in life and ministry whose encouragement after 33 years of marriage still amazes me. My children Edgar L. Vann, III and Ericka Monique Vann, who love me and make me proud every day.

To my staff, most especially, Rhonda Graves, my executive assistant and Kathy Pope, general manager of Edgar Vann ministries.

A special gratitude to Cathy Nedd who in so many ways made it happen.

I also acknowledge the Second Ebenezer and Ebenezer East family who inspired this work.

To God be the Glory

Preface

Taking command of your destiny is a way of looking at your life and looking at your future. We are in a day and a time when faith and the things that we have held dear in the body of Christ are under attack. We are living in a time, like never before, and we have to get ready.

Spiritually, during these times, we, as saints of God, have to be fortified so that we are in a position to go head to head, eyeball to eyeball, and toe to toe with the forces that come to derail our faith and to derail our destiny. This is something that we really have to watch, because the forces come in many forms. They come politically and they come economically. The forces come with such a great force that they cause even people of faith to lose heart.

Why do people of faith lose heart? People of faith often times lose heart because they are bombarded with negativity about their quality of life and what they can expect in the future.

God comes to offer you a future. What the devil comes to do is to get you to doubt your future. God comes to ensure that you are assured that he has plans for your future. What the devil comes to do is to try to make sure that you do not believe and that you doubt that there is any plan for you.

The way the devil gets you to doubt God's plan for you is by making sure that there are enough adverse circumstances around you to rob you of your destiny. Not because the devil can directly rob you – because he cannot, but because the devil understands the power of two elements that he knows can make inroads into your life. I believe that it is very important that you understand what those two elements are so that you can take command of our destiny.

Contents

CHAPTER 1

Thoughts and Words

"Prepare for the Battle!"

Everything in the universe begins with, revolves around and is given life and energy by two things – "thoughts" and "words." In fact, from the very beginning of time, everything in the universe revolved around two very seemingly simplistic things – thoughts and words.

For Satan to rob you of your destiny, he has to infiltrate, or infect your thought life, which manifests itself into what you say. He is not going to come and snatch the victory. By the time your victory comes, it is too late for Satan to do anything. He starts a lot earlier than that. Instead, he snatches the opportunity to speak into your thought life. Your thoughts become words. Your words become your belief system. And, your belief system brings your reality into existence whether it is good, or bad.

At all times, you must have on the whole armor of God. Otherwise, you are going to find yourself under attack and exposed. Do you know why the body of Christ is getting attacked now? The body of Christ is under attack because the world sees us rising. And, unlike many of us, the world understands where true power really resides. It understands that true power resides in the faith that people have in what they believe.

For example, America has difficulty dealing with terrorist, because of their very deep belief. No matter what you want to say about their beliefs, right or wrong, they believe it. I personally take issue with what they believe. However, they believe what they believe and they believe it enough that they will lay their life down for it.

The United States has never had enemies like it has today. World War I, World War II, Korea, Vietnam – we have had people who have fought us before, but we have not had people who believed. It is a very deep faith when people strap suicide bombs to themselves, and walk into a place because of their beliefs. I am telling you, we do not have any kind of artillery to fight that kind of extreme belief.

I am not saying it is a good thing – it is terrorism. What I am saying to you is that we do not have any kind of artillery or military to fight belief. Even the Bible says that when the people of God are strong, they will do great exploits.

The power to believe is the power that Satan cannot stand. He cannot deal with believers. He can deal with churchgoers, because many churchgoers do not believe in what they hear in church. For many churchgoers, the only reason why they are into the message is because it is good entertainment that releases them emotionally. But, when it gets to the point where it goes deeper than just their emotions and actually becomes a part of their thought-life and belief system, then Satan says, "Wait a minute. Hold it. I have to do something here. This is going too far."

When you begin to declare the Word that, *no weapon that is formed against you shall prosper,* (Isaiah 54:17) you begin to lay hold to precious promises that God has given to you that will allow you to be protected in times when the body of Christ is under attack.

Remember, everything in the universe begins with, revolves around and is given life and energy by two things – thoughts and words.

As the body of Christ, we must begin to understand that we are in a battle. We must understand that the Christian warfare is a fight. We must know that when we stand as children of God, timidity is no longer acceptable. Wishy washy, double-minded, jellyfish, unstable Christians are Satan's best advertisers. They are the sort of people who the devil wants to say see, "I got one here. I got one there. I got one over there and there and there." What he really likes to do is find Christians in prominent positions, so that he can point to them, derail them and cause others under them to lose faith.

Take spiritual leaders for example. In order to keep your faith strong, you had better believe God far beyond pastors. Don't get me wrong, they are pastors and spiritual leaders. They are a whole lot of things, but they are not your God. You should revere them and respect them. You should do a whole lot of things for them, because God placed them over you and gave them the privilege of speaking into your life. But if they fall, you have to keep standing, because the principles that they are teaching you are not of them. They are of God.

You can try the spirit, by the spirit and find out whether or not what they are teaching is the unadulterated Word of God. But it will remain the Word of God whether you fall, or your pastor falls, because the Word will still stand.

It is important that you understand that with the body under attack, whenever you go into the marketplace, in your job area, or wherever you may be, when you declare yourself to be a child of God, you are setting yourself up for attack.

Look at what happened to Mike Tyson, bless his heart. They catch him out at the bar, or out somewhere – dinner, or someplace, or wherever he goes for entertainment – and there are people there who say, "heavyweight champion, huh?" They decide that they are going to take a punch and pick a fight with Mike Tyson on the street so that they can get knocked out. Then they sue him.

What I am trying to say is that when you are a child of God, the world seeks to set you up. But, you have to be steadfast and unmovable and always abounding in the

Word of the Lord inasmuch as you know. You have to keep on serving God. If you do not realize this, you will not try to avoid the set up. If you don't know that you can be victorious over the set up, you will not try to avoid the set up.

> *Therefore, my beloved brethren, be ye steadfast, unmovable, always abounding in the work of the Lord, forasmuch as ye know that your labour is not in vain in the Lord.*
>
> \- *I Corinthians 16:58*

You should already know that you are a winner because your labor is not in vain in the Lord!

CHAPTER 2

The Power of Your Thought Life

"Creative Substance"

The power of your thought life began with the creativity of God. God conceived thoughts and then spoke things into existence. If you are a child of God, you have the same power to command your destiny.

Remember, you are not a human being seeking a spiritual experience. God did not create you that way. You are a spirit-being navigating through the human experience. You had a spirit before you had a body.

> *According as he hath chosen us in him before the foundation of the world, that we should be holy and without blame before him in love.*
>
> \- *Ephesians 1:4*

According to Ephesians 1:4, you were hanging out with God in eternity before your body got attached to it. So your birthday was really your earth day. It was the day that God decided to attach a body to your spirit which had already been with him in eternity.

When this body wears out, and it can no longer afford a dwelling place, you have a spirit that will not die. You have a body that will deteriorate, but a spirit that will not die. That spirit is going back to the same God that gave it to you in the first place, before he attached a body to it.

> *"In the beginning, God created the heaven and the earth.*
>
> *And the earth was without form, and void;…"*
>
> \- *Genesis 1:1 and 2*

Sometimes we attach the word form to void, but the earth was without form – AND void. There was nothing. Everything in its creative substance came through the Word of God.

These two elements – thoughts and words – form the creative substance that fills, molds and shapes your destiny. It is creative substance. Every thought that you have is creative substance. Every word that you utter is creative substance. This means that you need to watch your thoughts and watch your words.

Let's go back to Genesis.

> *"...and darkness was upon the face of the deep. And the spirit of God moved on the face of the waters.*
>
> *And God said, let there be light; and there was light."*
>
> \- *Genesis 1:2 - 3*

When God said, "Let there be light", this was something that was already a part of His creative mind. When you speak, whether it is consciously or unconsciously, you have already thought about what you are about to say - even people with diarrhea of the mouth. The problem with diarrhea is that you do not have any control over it, but it is already there. It just means you have lost control.

You have power in your words. More specifically, you have power over your thoughts that become your words. You need to be careful about what you say, especially if you have not thought about it. One thing that you ought to pray every day is, "Lord keep my mind clear." Do not let your mind get cluttered. If your mind gets cluttered, then your future is in jeopardy. You have to watch circumstances, because circumstances will cause your mind to get cluttered. Negative people in your space will cause your mind to get cluttered. And, sometimes, those are the very people who you love the most.

Take me for example, I personally like barbecue ribs. But, I cannot eat them because they are not good for me. Sometimes what you love the most may not be good for you. That is where you have to understand and say to yourself, "Am I trying to bring the future that God has for me?" This is about your destiny. Are you trying to bring your destiny closer to you? Or, are you bringing things closer to you that will rob you of what God wants you to have.

> *And God said let there be light and there was light and God saw the light and it was good. And God divided the light from the darkness.*
>
> \- *Genesis 1:4*

Once you do receive that which you do believe, you must properly appropriate it. There was light. Then

God divided light from darkness. Knowing how to use what you have is just as important as getting it.

> *For what shall it profit a man, if he shall gain the whole world and lose his soul?*
>
> \- *Mark 8:36*

It is important that you understand that you do not just want the blessing, but you want God to show you how to use the blessing.

Some people are just asking God for money as if that is the solution to their problems. In fact, they have had money and that probably was the beginning of their problems. How many folks have wasted money? I am talking about seasons of waste. I am not talking about one bad decision. How many people have gone through years of wasting what God had given to them?

It is not just getting it. It is how you appropriate it that is important. I can teach these principles. I can teach you how to think it, declare it and how to live in it. But, you have to learn how to appropriate it. That is why you have to keep praying. You know when you really have to start praying? It is when God gives you what you ask Him for.

God spoke light into existence. Light appeared, but light was never meant to stay on for 24 hours. Wisdom says that light is only designed to stay on for a specific time.

When God gives you a gift, you must know how to accurately appropriate it for the use in which it was intended. So it is important that you understand the context of how God gives it to you.

> *And God called the light Day, and the darkness he called Night. And the evening and the morning were the first day.*
>
> \- *Genesis 1:5*

Notice what God did. God did not go from morning to evening. He worked from evening to morning. The evening and the morning were the first day. God – the spirit – always works in darkness before things come to light. Things are always conceived in the spirit realm before they are manifested in the natural.

God did His best work in darkness. And, I have an announcement for anyone reading this book that is facing some dark times. I want you to be encouraged to know that God did His best work in darkness. In your toughest times, in your most challenging times, God is doing His greatest work. He brings morning out of your darkness. He does not bring darkness out of your morning. He brings light out of chaos. He brings light out of void and light out of abyss. He brings light out of nothing.

There are some who say, "You know what? I do not have much of anything anyway." Well, guess what, God's getting ready to bring you some light, because the evening and the morning are the first day.

> *And God said, Let there be a firmament in the midst of the waters, and let it divide the waters from the waters.*
>
> *And God made the firmament, and divided the waters which were under the firmament from the waters which were above the firmament and it was so.*
>
> \- *Genesis 1:6-7*

God made the firmament and divided the waters which were under the firmament and divided the waters which were above the firmament and it was so – why? Because he said it.

> *And God called the firmament heaven and the evening and the morning were the second day.*
>
> \- *Genesis 1:8*

God is still working from chaos into reality. Or, you could say, from chaos to cosmos. He is moving nothing to something.

> *And God said, let the waters under the heaven be gathered together unto one place, and let the dry land appear; and it was so.*
>
> \- *Genesis 1:9*

Thoughts and words form the creative substance that fills, molds and shapes your destiny. You have to watch your thoughts.

CHAPTER 3

The Blessing Is In Your Praise

"Command Your Soul to Praise Him"

For the weapons of our warfare are not carnal, but mighty through God to the pulling down of strong holds.

- *II Corinthians 10:4*

The weapons of our warfare are not carnal – meaning fleshly – but are mighty. We have mighty weapons. Do not think of yourself as nothing when God has called you mighty. Why are we mighty? We are mighty through God for the purpose of the pulling down of strongholds. Strongholds are pulled down, why? Because of the fight that we are in. The body is under attack. Our faith is under attack. The people of God are under attack.

The weapons that we fight with are not fleshly weapons. You will not solve an argument at work, for example, by cursing somebody out. They can probably out curse you any way – at least I hope they can. As a child of God, you ought not to be able to win a cursing contest.

The weapons of God are not fleshly. They are mighty through God for the pulling down of strongholds. The stronghold that is standing in the way of your destiny can be commanded to come down. Sometimes, you even have to command your soul to praise God, because maybe you got up on the wrong side of the bed. Maybe you are having a mood swing. Maybe there are some things going on that are coming up against you. The thing is that you have to command your soul to praise God. That is the sacrifice of praise.

The sacrifice of praise is praising God even when you don't really feel like it, or your heart is not into it. It is when you are in church, but you don't feel like shouting and praising Him. That is the very time that you need to learn how to command your soul to praise God.

The mood swing came because the devil did not want you to be in the mood to praise God. So if he can get you out of the mood, the disposition and the attitude that you should be praising God, then he can rob you of the blessings that come with praise. I hope you know that there are blessings that come with your praise. Praise brings blessings.

I know that you have been praying for some things, but there are some things that can be released by just praising God. That is why the very thing that the devil wants to do is to rob you of that praise. And, you let him rob you of your praise with any little old thing – somebody behind you whispering, or somebody unwrapping a piece of candy in church – and the next thing you know, you are distracted. It is at these times when you can command your soul to praise God.

As a matter of fact, command praise in your space. Do not even let the person sitting next to you destroy your praise. If they are not going to praise Him, it is just going to become an uncomfortable place for them to be. Do not let them distract you from your blessings. If anybody is going to get distracted, let it be them. If anybody is going to feel uncomfortable, let it be them.

Do not let anyone distract you and make you feel uncomfortable in your Father's house. God has been too good to you. So you can command your soul to praise Him because praise is tied to your destiny. It is tied to who you are. It is tied to what God wants to give you. It is tied to your well-being. So you can command your soul whenever you need to.

So, the next time you are in church and the people around you are acting like they do not feel the movement of the Lord, let them know that they can sit around and act funny if they want to. They can act like they have been inoculated with pickle juice if they want to. Let them know that your soul doth magnify the Lord.

You can pull strongholds down with your praise. As a matter of fact, praise is your weapon. It is certainly a weapon that the devil does not have. I personally like fighting the devil with a weapon that he does not have. I have praise and you do to. You can command your soul to praise Him.

CHAPTER 4

Casting Down Imaginations

"Wherever God is, His Power is There!

Casting down imaginations, and every high thing that exalteth itself against the knowledge of God, and bringing into captivity every thought to the obedience of Christ.

- *II Corinthians 10:5*

I like the word imaginations because it really indicates that anything that God did not say, is not true. It is just something you are imagining. As a matter of fact, even when you are looking at something – though you cannot deny that it exists – *you can call things that be not as though they were.* (Romans 4:17) You cannot call things that are as though they are not. You cannot deny the existence of certain things, but you can align yourself with a power that is greater than what you can see.

So if you are looking at lack, do not deny it, but do not accept it either. Do not accept it as your fate, because that is not where you are permanently. If you are not in a place where you can take care of yourself, it is not permanent. It is transitional. You are not in a place where you cannot be free. If you are bound, those shackles are about to be loose because you have to be set free so that you can reach the destiny that God has for you.

You have to cast down imaginations and every high thing. I like the word "high" because a lot of times, the world will put high things in front of you. It will put great things in front of you – great opportunities. Whenever people commit a crime – first of all they thought about it. But secondly, when it is presented to other folk – their accomplices – it was presented as a high thing. "We can get away with it, man. We can do this, right?"

You are supposed to be able to say you *can do all things through Christ which strengthens me*. (Philippians 4:13) But, we sometimes allow the world to get in the middle of that and we figure that we need the world system to validate what God wants to give us.

You have to *rebuke every high thing that exalts itself against the knowledge of God.* (2 Corinthians 10:5) How do you know what is against God? You have to know the Word of God. If you do not know the Word of God, you do not know what exalts itself against the Word of God. If you do not know the Word of God, you do not know what is real and what is fake. You do not know real people from fake people.

You have to pray to the Lord to give you a spirit of discernment so that you know real people from people who are phony. That does not mean that you are not going to work with phony people. That does not mean that you will not relate to some phony folks. It does not mean that you will not have to deal with some phony folks. What it means is, "Lord help me know the difference so that I know how to deal." You need God's help so that you know what to say and how to say it.

Ask God to help you so that you do not get so emotionally attached to people that Satan has dispatched to destroy and derail your destiny. I am not saying that you should stop speaking to people and stop being nice.

But I say unto you, Love your enemies, bless them that curse you, do good to them that hate you, and pray for them which despitefully use you, and persecute you.

- *Matthew 5:44*

Wisdom is the principal thing; therefore get wisdom; and with all thy getting get understanding.

- *Proverbs 4:7*

You have power to command things that come against your spiritual thought life. You have power to cast those things down. High things exalt up, but we are able to bring them down. Strongholds take place up, but we are able to pull them down. We pull them down and they have no preeminence. They have no power.

You can cast down imaginations and things that exalt themselves against the knowledge of God bringing them into captivity. You can put under arrest every thought so that it might be made conformable to God and the obedience of Christ. You can bring your thoughts into alignment with what God's Word says.

When you bring your thoughts into alignment with what His Word says and you are in agreement with Him – *where two, or three are gathered together* touching hands, it is the power of agreement. Agreeing when He says, *I am a God in the midst.* (Matthew 18:20) If He is in the midst, His presence is there. If His presence is there, His power is there. And, if His power is there, His provisions are there.

You have the power to be able to command your destiny through your thought life. You can bring your thoughts into captivity when they are not what they should be – when you sublimely think of things that you know are violating the laws of God. You have the power to subvert these thoughts and to bring them under captivity – arrest – unto the obedience of Christ.

You have power over your thoughts. Remember, everything in the universe begins with, revolves around and is given life and energy by thoughts and words.

CHAPTER 5

The Fundamental Principles of God

"A Quest to Arrive at the Place God Intended"

It is so important that you understand the fundamental principles of God's Word, because when you are guided by the principles of God's Word, you are guided by the root of God's Word.

You cannot live by your shout. Your shout is really the by-product of the principles that you adhere to. It is a visible showing that you believe the promises that God has made so clearly to you. But your shout alone is not enough to live by. Your shout comes after you have adhered to the principles that God has given to you so that you understand how to live your life.

How to live your life is so very, very important, because what we need now are principles, concepts and strategies to enhance the quality of our lives. The emotion comes and the anointing comes and we flow with that anointing. We flow with that emotion and all of that is good, but you have to have principles to live by. You have to have time-tested, God-revealed principles to live by so that your life is in accordance with the Word of God, so that your steps are ordered by the Lord.

When your steps are ordered by the Lord, then you find out that God has a destiny for you. Of course, the root word of destiny is the same root word for the word destination, which means that destiny is really the quest that you have to arrive at the place God intended for you. When I say place, I am not talking about geography. When I say place, I am talking about the spiritual place. The place intended for you to be.

The fundamental principle for this teaching is that everything in the universe begins with, revolves around and is given life and energy by our thoughts and words. There are thoughts and words involved in everything that takes place in the universe. They form the creative substance that fills, molds and shapes your destiny, and we have already defined destiny as your quest to arrive at the place God intended for you to be.

Can you say truthfully that you know that where you are is not your arrival point. Can you say with confidence that you are still being transported to destiny. And, that destiny has not fully arrived for you yet. Actually, you are in certain segments of your destiny. You are performing certain things that are a part in the continuum of your destiny. But as for your destiny – the intended place – you are not there yet. You are working on it, but you are not there yet because God is still working on you.

I want you to look beyond the accumulation of material things as your destiny. You have to understand that your destiny is an intended spiritual place where God intends for you to be – which does not necessarily relate at all to how much money you have.

There are some people who are broke, but fulfilling destiny. There are some people who do not have what they wish they could have, but they are walking presently in destiny because they are at the intended place where God wanted them to be. They are doing the intended thing with the intended purpose that God has for them in their lives.

It is not about how much money you have. A lot of people say they are not where they want to be because they are not in the house they want to be in. It does not matter who you are, you are not in the house you want to be in. You are not in your final house. You are not driving your last car. I do not care how nice your house is. Do not ever look at that as being all God can do for you. It does not matter how nice your car is. Do not ever look at that as being all God can do for you.

A good case in point - Bill Gates is the richest man in America. He is worth – on a good Wall Street day – upwards of $60 billion. You may think that his destiny was to come up with Microsoft, one of the most widely used software systems in the world. You may think that was his destiny and that he has already fulfilled it.

But, I beg to differ because what Bill Gates has really found at this particular point in his life is that everything he has, all of his success and all of the monetary wealth that he has accumulated was only preparing him for what is probably now the destiny moment in his life. Because of his wealth, he can now go into African nations and transform them – not one person at a time, not one block at a time, but one nation at a time. People who were hungry are being fed. People who had AIDS are being treated. People who did not have water are getting water.

The computer was the passageway by which he accumulated what he needed in order to really fulfill his destiny. Had he just gotten all wrapped up in getting money, then he would have quit living a long time ago. God wakes you up every morning for a purpose. You are not waking up every morning to continue to recite to yourself, "I made it, I made it, I made it. I do not need to do anything else, my living is made." God did not let you live for that. He wakes you up every morning for you to understand that you are here for an intended purpose. I do not care how successful you were yesterday; it is not enough for what he has for you today.

Know that what is coming is better. Know that what is in the future is better. The more you lean towards what your future holds for you, the more you understand that today was just a prelude in the continuum of the journey of where God has intended for you to be -- because that is your destiny. Your destiny is your having a quest for that which God has ordained for your life.

Destiny is a quest to arrive at the intended place that God has in store for you. You should always look to what God has in store for you with anticipation and hope. You should always look to the future to see something – to believe God for something that you do not necessarily see today. If all you can believe God for is what you can believe him for today then you might as well quit today. You are living so that what you believe him for tomorrow will be greater than what you believe him for today.

Everything rises and falls, begins, revolves around and gets life and energy from your thoughts and your words.

> *For I know the thoughts that I think toward you, saith the Lord, thoughts of peace and not of evil, to give you an expected end.*
>
> \- *Jeremiah 29:11*

God has a destiny in mind for you. God says that he has things in mind as it relates to you. He says that he has you on His mind. You are not lost in the realm of divine thought. You are on his mind. He has things that He is working on in your behalf. That is why you cannot give up even though sometimes you feel like giving up. God says that he has things in mind that you have not yet seen and that have not yet been revealed to you. He has things concealed that are yet to be revealed.

However, they are not going to be revealed until he gets through working on them. They are not going to be revealed until he can bring about the proper time and place for you to receive them. Not that he has to work on something, but he has to work on you. He has to get you straight because he has to get you to understand. He has to put you in a place where you can appreciate some things. He has to put you in a place where when he blesses you – you are a good steward of it, which means he might have to let you slip and fall a couple of times.

It is like when you teach a child how to ride a bike and you get behind them and push them. You are pushing them and holding the bike up. You are running alongside of them. They think that you are still with them, but they do not know that you have let the bike go. You have to let the bike go a couple of times and let them skin a couple of knees and elbows. Then you have to kiss the elbow and put a band aid on it. They had to get some cuts on their elbows in order to get back up and get encouraged. They had to be told to get back on the bike and try it again.

God has to do you that way in life sometimes until you are ready for it. He has to work on you. He has to put you on the bike and walk right beside you. Then he has to let you go a little bit and let you flap your wings on your own a little bit. Then he watches you lovingly as you fall every now and then and skin a few knees and get a few heartaches and a few disappointments and a little hardship. Then he says aha! I can trust them now because they know that I am here for them. They know that they do not have to worry about it.

Have you been through some things in your life that were really set ups for the real stuff that God wanted you to have? You thought it was such a bad thing. You thought it was so bad and that it was so rough. "Why would God let me suffer like this? Why would he let me go through this?" As a matter of fact, it is bad when you start going through stuff over and over again. You say – "that happened to me once, but I am sure not going to let it happen to me again."

Then you turn around and it happens to you again and you are embarrassed. You are looking around and saying this should not have ever taken place. You should not have ever been dealing with this again. You promised yourself it would never happen. You promised yourself you would not go through this again and somehow or another here you are.

But, you get on your knees and you say, "Lord, this does not make any sense whatsoever." And somehow, some kind of way, you have to learn your lesson this time and move from where you are to where He intended you to be. That is when you know that God is moving you toward your destiny.

He has plans for you – plans of good, not evil. He has thoughts that he thinks toward you. And, for anything to happen in your life, it has to be from a divine thought. He has always made something a reality in the spirit realm – in the realm of His divine thought – before it gets down to the natural realm. Something always exists in the spirit before it comes out in the flesh. Before your reality actually comes, understand that thoughts and words had to make it happen.

So it is very important that you understand this in the true context of what God has decided and ordained for your life and your destiny.

CHAPTER 6

Words Have Power

"Watch God Transform Your Life!"

Your words have power. Say it aloud to yourself, "My words have power." Before you allow anything, as it relates to the Word of God, to snatch that Word out of you, you have to be able to declare that Word in you. I am talking about words. Words are very, very important. So, you have to speak some words over yourself.

> *So then faith cometh by hearing, and hearing by the word of God.*
>
> \- *Romans 10:17*

You have to even hear yourself say the Word of God. You get more faith when you begin to say the Word yourself. So speak up. Do not deny yourself the blessing that the Lord has in store for you.

> *How forcible are right words! But what doth your arguing reprove?*
>
> - *Job 6:25*

How potent are right words. The phrase "right words" presupposes that evidently there must be some wrong words. If there are right words and if the scripture says that right words are forcible, powerful and potent, it evidently means that wrong words have the opposite effect. Surely, you can glean that.

In other words, if there are right words, there must be wrong words. If right words have forced power, and potency, evidently wrong words have the opposite effect. So, when you begin speaking words over yourself that are negative, you lose the potency of what right words would do for you. How powerful, how potent, how forcible are right words.

The words you say have power. Why? Because your inner world creates your outer world. What is inside of you is creating something outside of you.

"For as he thinketh in his heart, so is he…"

- Proverbs 23:7

When you think and then you speak, you speak words that are creative. God used a word to create. God said, "Let there be light" and light came skipping out of the closets of nowhere into existence. Why? Because God said it. He spoke it and it came to pass.

I believe you will start speaking some things and you will start seeing some things change in your life. The problem is that you have been praying it, but you have not been speaking it. You have been hearing other people talk about it. You are waiting for a word from somebody else, but God is saying I am waiting for you to recite the same words that I put in your belly. You are waiting for somebody else to say something over you that is supposed to transform your life, but it really does not mean anything if you do not adhere to it and point yourself in the direction of the Word that has been spoken over your life.

I can say it over and over again, but if you do not internalize it, you will not get it. All you will have is a nice book and you will say, "This sure is good." That is not enough for me. You do not want something that is just good on the outside. You should want something that is going to transform you on the inside. You need to internalize it. You need a Word that you are going to take in. You do not just need to hear a word. You need to be able to internalize the Word that you can speak over your life.

Right words have power. They have strength. You may not have anything, but you have words. Your closet may not be full, but you have words. You may not have a pair of shoes in every shoe box that you have, but you have words. Open up your mouth and speak words of life over yourself and over your family.

When your children are asleep walk to the door and lay your hands on the door. Speak words of life over them when they do not even see you – when they do not even feel that you are there. They will get up and say, "Mama, there has to be a God somewhere, because things are different today than they were yesterday." And you'll say, "I know they are because I have been speaking something over your life."

The hymnologist wrote:

And he walks with me,
And He talks with me,
And He tells me I am His own;
And the joy we share as we tarry there,
None other has ever known.

He speaks, and the sound of His voice,
Is so sweet the birds hush their singing,
And the melody that He gave to me
Within my heart is ringing.

Jesus is speaking and you have to learn how to line up with what he is saying. When you begin to speak what he speaks, your words have power. They create substance.

> *Now faith is the substance of things hoped for, the evidence of things not seen.*
>
> \- *Hebrews 11:1*

You know what substance is? Substance – sub strata – is the thing under you that holds you when it looks like you are standing on nothing. Faith is the substance. It is the thing under you that is standing you up when there is not anything under you to stand you up. Those are forcible right words.

Thou art snared with the words of thy mouth, thou art taken with the words of thy mouth.

- *Proverbs 6:2*

Now, what does snared mean? Snared means that you are caught – attached. You are captive by the words of your mouth. You are defined by what you say. You cannot become something that you did not say you can become. You are snared by it. You are defined by it.

The best-selling author and leadership expert John Maxwell says something very revealing about the Law of the Lid. He says that you really do not rise up very far above where you think you can rise. You will not rise too far above your own expectation. You are going to end up just about the level where your words and thoughts collide, which means that a whole lot of us have a lot of talking up to do.

Take a journal of yourself and start noticing the stuff you say. It is like when you are on one of those fad diets and you have to write down everything that you eat. On about the third day, you just give up. You give up because you have convinced yourself that you do not have to write certain things down. Just a candy bar – my God – why put that down? You warmed up some barbecue ribs that you had left over and only ate four bones – that is all you ate; along with that little piece of chicken you still had from Sunday.

You have to be very careful because when you start taking a word inventory and you start looking at the things that you say – the stuff that comes out of your mouth – you begin to understand then that there is a whole lot of stuff that should not have been said.

You have to watch people who talk too much, because either they start talking about people, or they talk too much about themselves. Unless you are a walking encyclopedia, the average person does not have that kind of knowledge base to be able to address every subject. They could not possibly have something to say about anything and everything.

Many people who talk a lot are either talking about two things – themselves, or other people. How much of that is edifying? You do not want to hear them talk about themselves all day, because that gets tiring. Every time they talk – every time they open their mouths, it is all about them, them, them, I, I, I, me, me, me.

You do not want people in your life who are always talking about other folks all the time either. "Did you see?" "Have you heard?" "Well it looks like to me..." You need to say, "I have another appointment I will talk to you later." You are snared by the words of your mouth. You are defined by what your mouth says.

The Word of the Lord says that your circumstance should never define your consciousness, but your consciousness should always define your circumstance. Do not allow what you are looking at to define you. As a matter of fact, you have to be in a position to speak something different than what you see.

If you do not have any words forcibly to speak something different than what you see, then you have to learn how to deal with disagreeable people without becoming disagreeable yourself. You cannot become disagreeable because that is what you see.

Sometimes, you have to be around people who have low self-esteem, bad expectations of themselves, on guilt trips, power trips and all kinds of stuff. But you do not have to become what you see. You have a destiny. You have a quest to reach an intended place in God. It is very important to stay focused on the things that God has ordained for your life.

You are snared by the words of your mouth. You are taken with the words of your mouth. You are actually caught and taken by the things that you say. Sometimes, as soon as stuff comes out of your mouth, it happens. Have you ever been talking about a person who you have not seen in a long time, and as soon as you mention their name, they come around?

I know this has happened at least once or twice in your lifetime. You called them up. As a matter of fact, you will even go so far as to tell someone else, "Now, do not call that name, because they might appear."

You want God to be pleased with your words. You want the things that are uttered out of your mouth to be pleasing in His sight. You want to synchronize God's Will with your desire. You want what God wants for you. Your life would be a whole lot better if you just synchronized your will with God's Will. Then, you will get to a point where you are actually seeking to get to that intended place that He has ordained for your life. You do not really want to be caught outside of the center of His Will.

CHAPTER 7

Spiritual Maturity

"It's Not All About You"

It takes spiritual maturity to get to that intended place – your destiny. A part of your spiritual maturation process is for you to be able to look at your life and look at yourself and recognize that you are really not where you need to be, spiritually. A lot of times you are not there financially, because you are not there spiritually. You are not there emotionally, or relationally because you are not there spiritually. God is not yet ready to trust you with that which you cannot be trusted.

Let's examine something very basic, like relationships. Some people cannot be trusted with a relationship, because they are too selfish. In other words, they do not have a spirit of sharing. It is all me, myself and I. And,

God says, "I am not going to give you anyone then. If it is all about you, stay that way. When you get tired of it, come back and see me."

In any relationship, you have to learn that you do not get to have your way all of the time. Things are not the way you would like them to be all of the time. When you come to understand this, you begin to look at yourself analytically and realize that you can adjust, especially if there is a bond of trust in the relationship. You come to understand that sometimes, it has to be the way the other person wants it to be because the two of you are in this thing together.

Many people do not have constructive relationships in their lives. I am talking about relationships with others. For some, the problem is that your personality is not conducive to any kind of relationship because you have so many hang-ups and so many issues. You have so many unrecognized and unaddressed needs for validation and affirmation that every time you get hooked up with something, or someone, everything has to be just like you want it to be.

Let me just tell you, life is not Burger King. You cannot have it your way all the time. There are going to be rules and regulations. There are going to be things that you have to adhere to. God has to sometimes work on you and get you to the point where you say, "Lord whatever your Will is for me, that is what I want in my life." It may not feel good, or look right. It may not make sense to you. Or, you may wish it would have been another way. But somehow God is showing you something in the middle of it and you are learning a lesson.

You are learning how to wait on God. You are learning how to take a licking and keep on ticking. You are learning how to adjust. You are learning how to do this thing. For sure, one thing you have learned is that it is not going to be the way that you want it to be all the time.

> *Let the words of my mouth, and the meditation of my heart be acceptable in thy sight, O Lord, my strength, and my redeemer.*
>
> \- *Psalms 19:14*

You are going to need some strength because when it is not like you want it to be, you have a tendency to get upset and start acting out. This is when you need God's strength so that you do not make a bigger fool of yourself. You need God's strength so that you do not behave like a six year old when you do not get your way. You are in an adult body, but you are still acting like a school kid.

God is your strength. When you do not get your way, God is your strength. When you cannot see how things are going to happen, God is your strength. Have you ever had something inside of you that keeps telling you that everything is going to be all right even though you are looking at the situation and it does not appear as though it is ever going to be right? But, somehow God makes it right, because he says in your spirit, "It is going to be all right."

You can stop being angry, because it is going to be all right. You do not have to be in a rage, because it is going to be all right. You can stop taking things the wrong way all of the time, because it is going to be all right. God is your strength. He is your redeemer. What is a Redeemer? A Redeemer is one who has brought you back.

When I was a kid, we would get these stamps every time we went to the grocery store. At that time, there were two kinds of stamps – S&H Green Stamps and Gold Bell Stamps. Based on how much you spent at the store, you would get a certain amount of stamps.

My mother also had these books. She would spend a lot of time sitting up at night in the kitchen with a glass of water. She would dip her finger in the water, put the water on the page of the books, moisten the page, take the stamps, stick them on the page and then fill the books up.

Then, she would take the books filled with stamps to a place known as a redemption center. She would say to me, "Boy, get these books and put them in the car on the back seat because we are going down to the Green Stamp redemption center." I would say, "What are we doing taking all these silly books anywhere." She would say, "Boy, just do what I say." So I would put the books on the back seat of the car and go down to the redemption center with my mother.

Now, behind the counter, at the redemption center, there were things that we could buy with the stamps that we had collected as a reward for the transactions that we had made.

Just like exchanging those stamps for a reward, God is your Redeemer because he has rewards waiting for you. Your reward is not based upon your ability. It is not based upon who you are, or how fine you think you are. It is not based on anything like that. Your rewards are based upon the transactions of life that you have been through. They are based on the ups and the downs and the ins and outs that you have been through.

I want to suggest that what you are going through right now is just stamps in your redemption center. They are stamps that God wants you to collect for your experiences. You can collect for the things that are going on in your life because He is your strength; He is your Redeemer.

The words of your mouth and the meditations of your heart have to be made acceptable in the eyesight of God.

CHAPTER 8

Speak Words of Authority

Transform Your Life

Your words with authority bring life and energy. Let me repeat this, your words when they are laden with authority bring life and energy.

> *And when Jesus was entered into Capernaum, there came unto him a Centurion beseeching him.*
>
> *And saying Lord, my servant lieth at home sick of the palsy, grievously tormented.*
>
> \- *Matthew 8:5-6*

When Jesus came into Capernaum, he was met by a Centurion. A Centurion was a soldier, but not just any soldier. A Centurion was a ranking officer in the army who had 100 men assigned to him in a battalion. It is also important to point out that he was a Roman Centurion. He was not a Jew, but he was a part of the Roman army. I point this out, because a key factor of this Bible story is that this Roman Centurion – a man with great authority – beseeches Jesus, who was a Jew.

The Roman Centurion says to Jesus, a Jew:

> *Lord my servant lieth home paralyzed and grievously tormented.*
>
> \- *Matthew 8:6*

First of all, he calls him Lord. You can call him Savior when he saves you. But, a whole lot of people cannot call him Lord. Lord means ruler. It means dominion. When you call him Lord that means you are going to do what he says. When you call him Lord that means you are going to live by what he wants you to live by.

The Centurion says, *"Lord my servant lies…"* You have to understand the culture of the text. You have to understand that he, as a Centurion, hardly ever spoke to his servants, but he had compassion for his servant. His servant was not a Roman. His servant was also a Jew.

Anecdotally, I believe that God has some extra points for folk who routinely pray for other folks just as hard as they pray for themselves. I believe that God gets tired of this me, me, me, prayer all of the time. Because after a while God sees that your only focus is you. Are you concerned about other people?

The servant was not somebody in the Centurion's family. He was not somebody in his running crowd. The servant was a person – especially based on the classism of the day – who was completely in a slave class under the Centurion. But the Centurion still says to Jesus, *"my servant lies sick of palsy, paralyzed and grievously tormented."*

Jesus responds that he is going to come heal the servant, but he never gets to the Centurion's house. Actually, he does not have to go to the house. Why? Because he is already at the house. He is at my house, even though I am not at my house right now. He is at your house, even though you may not be home right now. He is at our houses keeping them safe until we get back there.

Even when we get back there, he keeps us safe while we are there. When we go to sleep at night, He keeps us safe. He is omnipresent. He is where you are right now and he is at your house.

The Centurion answers Jesus in verse 8:

> *…and said, Lord, I am not worthy that thou shouldest come under my roof, but speak the Word only, and my servant shall be healed.*
>
> *For I am a man under authority, having soldiers under me: and I say to this man, Go, and he goeth; and to another, Come, and he cometh; and to my servant, Do this, and he doeth it.*
>
> \- *Matthew 8:8, 9*

Now, just imagine, here is a Centurion – a Roman Centurion who has never been in the synagogue. He does not observe the worship traditions of the Jews. He is not a person who is wrapped up in Jesus' way of thinking. But he knows that Jesus is God in the flesh. He knows that if anybody can heal his servant, Jesus can. But he has a different frame of reference.

He knows that he is a man of authority, who is under authority, and he has people under his authority. But he knows that in order to have people under him, he has to have people over him, because it is the people over him who gives him the authority with the people under him.

Let me explain it in a different way. You are in trouble when you are under somebody who is not under somebody else. For example, it does make a difference what church you belong to, because everybody is not under authority. The only way you can exert authority is to be under authority.

The Centurion said listen I know how that works because I have people under me. If I tell them go do this, they do it. If I tell them go fetch that, they do it. If I tell them go, they go. If I tell them come, they come. If I tell my servant to do something, my servant does exactly what it is I say to him because I know the authority and the power of words.

So the Centurion says to Jesus, I tell you what you do. You do not have to come under my roof, because I am not worthy anyway. He says, "If you, sir could but just speak it." That is why I ask the Lord to speak to my heart. He says, "Lord if you could just speak it. I know that it is difficult, but Lord, if you would just speak it, I know it will be all right."

In other words, Lord, if you would just tell me that I am going in the right direction. If you would just tell me that my steps are ordered by you. The hardest thing is to trust God when nothing has changed. But you can trust him when nothing has changed if He speaks the Word and tells you that you are going in the right direction.

How many times have you stopped at the gas station for directions when you were lost and they said you were going in the right direction. They tell you to just stay on the right road. Then when you get back in the car and look at that road again, it starts looking better. It starts looking better because you have a word that tells you that you are on the right road.

The Centurion knew that all God had to do was to speak a word and his servant would be healed. He was a man under authority. He knew the power of words. Words have power. Words have authority.

> *When Jesus heard it, he marveled, and said to them that followed. Verily I say unto you, I have not found so great faith, no, not in Israel.*
>
> \- *Matthew 8:10*

When you speak words, speak not only of authority, but of faith. God responds only to faith. That is what the Word says. He empathizes with your tears, but your tears have no creative power. He dries your tears, He comforts you and He comes to see about you. But your tears do not have any power to change anything. Your emotions do not change anything either. It is your faith that changes things. Even your prayers have to have faith attached to them in order to change things.

Do not just go through the motion and emotion of prayer. You had better have some faith attached to it. Otherwise, just reciting good prayers will not change one thing in your life if you do not have faith to believe and speak the words you speak from a place of authority and power.

Jesus said, "I have not found this kind of faith." He basically says, I can respond to faith like this with my remote control. I do not have to come to your house. I do not have to follow you home. Your faith is enough for me to declare to you that your servant is going to be healed. Now, you just go on back home. I am not coming. I am not laying on hands. I do not have any oil. I am just going to come when I get ready. But, I am not coming now.

All I am going to do is speak the Word only. If you have the kind of faith that God can speak a Word into your life that is going to transform your very existence, then your quality of life is going to be transformed by the power of God. Just learn how to speak the Word only.

You have to speak His Word no matter how things look and no matter what other people say. It does not matter how dark the day gets, speak His Word. Speak it. Do not relent from what God has said unto you. Open your mouth and declare it in Jesus' name.

Speak the Word and whatever God says, that is what you should believe. Speak it over your situation. Speak it over your life. Speak it over your family, your children, your grandchildren, your co-workers, neighbors, people in the community, folk in the church, world situations, personal turmoil, and destiny opportunities. Speak it over everything and everyone. Speak it!

If you do this, God is going to show up in a mighty way. Speak the Word; and in that same hour, people are going to be healed. People are going to be saved. People are going to be delivered if you speak the Word only. And God has ordained that those that speak and live the Word shall be guided by the Word.

Speak God's Word and you will be on your way to your destiny. God has great things in store for you, because your destiny is an intended place that God has for you. God wants you to follow Him to your destiny. He wants you to follow him to your intended place. Follow Him to your wealthy place. Follow Him to your blessing. Follow Him to your place of healing. Follow Him and you will be on your way somewhere.

Declare that your faith is taking you somewhere. Take command of your destiny. Do not leave your future to chance. Take it. The devil does not want you to have it, but take it.

> *The Kingdom of God suffereth violence, and the violent take it by force.*
>
> \- *Matthew 11:12*

Take it! Nobody is going to give it to you. You have to take it. Your faith is going to have to take it. If you wait on friends, you will never get there. If you wait on kinfolk, you will never get there. If you wait on coworkers, you will never get there. If you wait on colleagues, you will never get there. Your faith has to take some stuff, but you can take command of your destiny and watch God transform your life by the words that you say.

CHAPTER 9

Speak the Right Words

"Take Your Life Back!"

The name of the Lord is a strong tower: the righteous runneth into it, and is safe.

- *Proverbs 18:10*

We are thankful that we have faith in the Word. There is safety in the Word. There is Power in the Word. There is healing in the Word. There is direction in the Word. There is purpose in the Word. God's intentionality is in the Word. So we are excited about the Word of the Lord.

This is extremely essential as it pertains to how you take command of your destiny. How you begin to walk in destiny. How you begin to take authority over circumstances and begin to make life manageable.

For life to be manageable, you must understand that life goes through several cycles. As you go through life you are always going through cycles. There are stages, there are eras, there are dispensations of your life that you go through, on a regular basis, that help you to understand the full spectrum of life and how it continues to unfold for you.

So, it is important that life becomes manageable. So far, we have talked about the things that help you create your world. The things that help to define who you are. The things that help to define your future and your present.

It is important that you know that if you are going to take command of your destiny, you should never take command of something that you are not familiar with. You cannot take command of something that you are not comfortable with. You cannot take command of something for which you feel that you have no power, or authority to direct.

So, if your life is unmanageable, and you cannot take command of your destiny, then you are not living your life. For example, if there are things in your life that have you frustrated, conflicted, confused and depressed all the time, then you are not ready to take command of anything. First, you are going to have to take your life back. You are going to have to ask God to help you take your life back.

Many people that we know do not have command over their own lives. Their own lives are elusive to them. They do not really have it together. They are dealing with all kinds of circumstances and moving in all kinds of directions.

So, how do we deal with this? We have been talking about how thoughts and words define us. How our inner world creates our outer world. We have been talking about how the things inside of us shape the things outside of us. How destiny is created, shaped, formed and fashioned by the things that go on inside of us. We have been talking about how these things help to create what needs to happen outside of us.

I hope you have begun to understand that there are two things that you have power over inside of you that define what goes on outside of you. These are two things that God has given to you – no matter what your circumstances are and no matter how tough things seem. No matter what you are looking at or what your reality seems to be externally, you find out that internally everything in the universe begins with, revolves around and is given life and energy by thoughts and words.

We also begin to know and understand that our thoughts and our words are under our control. We have power and authority over our thoughts and our words. It is important that you understand this because the Bible says:

> *For the weapons of our warfare are not carnal, but mighty through God to the pulling down of strong holds.*
>
> *Casting down imaginations, and every high thing that exalteth itself against the knowledge of God, and bringing into captivity every thought to the obedience of Christ;*
>
> \- *II Corinthians 10:4-5*

You have the power and the authority in the Word of God to channel your thought patterns and to channel your words. You can cast down imaginations. Imaginations are those things that rise against the knowledge of God itself. So anything that does not line up with God's Word is an imagination. It is not real. It is imagined. It may be fact, but it is not the truth. So you have to glean the truth. The truth helps you to understand that you have on your side the power inside of you, creatively, to create that outer world with what you say.

That which you say has power and it has potency, so you need to watch what you say, because, if you want great things to happen and to flourish in your life, you need to be concerned about what you say. You have to know that for things to begin to flourish in your life, you have to say the right words.

The right words have to be in the atmosphere helping you to create on the outside of you that which you can conceive and imagine on the inside. It is your thoughts and your words. Again, everything in the universe begins with, revolves around and is given life and energy by thoughts and words.

It is important that we understand that our words are living organisms. They are living epistles that help us to begin to shape the things around us. The Bible says in Proverbs 3:23, *"As a man thinketh in his heart, so is he."* We become what we think and we become what we say. Paul said in Romans:

> *That if thou shalt confess with thy mouth the Lord Jesus, and shalt believe in thine heart that God hath raised him from the dead, thou shalt be saved.*
>
> \- *Romans 10:9*

So, it is your words that save you. If you shall confess with the mouth of the Lord Jesus and believe in your heart that raised Him from the dead, he said that thou shall be saved. But, with the mouth confession is made.

> *For with the heart man believeth unto righteousness; and with the mouth confession is made unto salvation.*
>
> \- *Romans 10:10*

Being saved had to do with your words. As you confessed Him you were saved. So if your words define you spiritually, they define you in every other way. Your words define your salvation – your ultimate relationship with God. They define who you are in Him. They define whether you are going to live eternally in heaven, or hell. They define whether or not you are going to leave here and go home with Him after this life is over, then words have power to create some other stuff in your life.

It is important that you understand that thoughts and words are vitally important as it relates to your destiny.

CHAPTER 10

Connect to God's Order

"Be Careful How You Do Things"

I want to introduce another principle that I think is pertinent to your thoughts and words. That is the principle of order. You have thoughts and words, but you must also have them connected to God's Order. You have thoughts and words, but you must have your thoughts and words under subjection.

If your thoughts and words are not under subjection, what begins to happen is that you violate God's order. And, when you violate God's order, it renders your words and your thoughts null and void. It is important that you understand that your life has to be in order and that you have to have the things in order that are pertinent to your destiny.

Let me define order as a principle. Order is the regulation of a prevailing course, or arrangement of things that reinforce the intent of God. You understand the intent of God because the intent of God is reinforced by the prevailing order, or divine arrangement of things. In other words, order is God's regulation and not yours.

The problem that we have is that we want to regulate everything ourselves. We want to be in total control. You will find in your life that there are times when things are totally out of your hands. They are out of your control. I want you to know that God sends these times in your life for a purpose. The purpose is that you may not get so high minded and think that you are all that to the point where you do not need God.

God sends these times to make sure that you stay reliant upon Him. And, that your faith stays intact. God knows that the only way your faith can stay intact is that He has to throw some stuff in the game. He has to turn some stuff all upside down.

Have you ever been at a point where your life is going like a washing machine with stuff going every which way? You wonder if you can keep the lid on it so that you will not be embarrassed. You are trying to sit on this thing and keep the lid on it so that everyone does not have to see all of your business.

God wants you in a place sometimes where you are so discombobulated that you do not have anything else you can do except say, "Lord, I need you. I need your direction. I need you to order my steps. If you do not order my steps, I do not know where I am going to go. I do not know what I am going to do. I am going to just stand right here until I receive direction from you."

God will throw you off. He will tweak some things in your life. He will push some buttons in your life and you will get to the point where you wonder when things are going to settle down. When are things going to be comfortable? God sometimes says that you are going to have to deal with discomfort so that He can get you ready for this next level that you keep asking Him for.

You are going to have to learn how not to be in control and how not to be a person that you think is so great. You are going to have to learn how to condescend sometimes. You are going to have to learn how not to be so happy with yourself. You are going to have to learn how not to be so conceited. You are going to have to learn how not to be so self-assured. God is going to put a little glitch in your step. He is going to mess your stride up for a minute.

God says you have been so used to your little strut that He is going to have to cut your strut just a little bit. He can bring your strut a little bit down so that you cannot strut like you used to. Then you will look at the one who gave you the strut in the first place.

God is calling for order. God says He wants to be the regulator. If you are doing what you are doing for your own satisfaction, then that is just for you. That is your reward. But if you are doing what you are doing for Him to get the glory, you had better start listening to how He wants it done. He doesn't want His stuff done any kind of way. He does not want it done your way. He wants you to get it done His way.

You see, when we are out of order, things in our lives begin to go wrong. When we are out of order, you can tell. When a few things are bad for you, you are conflicted, upset and in a tizzy. Every week you have another concern and you are sending out emails to your friends. If that is what is going on in your life, you need to check your life because; evidently, you are deficient in some area of order.

Order is God's regulation. It is the regulation of a prevailing course, or arrangement of things that are designed to reinforce the intent of God. It is you submitting yourself to God's intent. So you want your thoughts and your words to line up with the intent of God, which means you have to know His Will.

The only way to know His Will is to know His Word. His Will is in His Word and His Word is His Will. A lot of times you try to make God's Will something that you want it to be. God says you have to check with Him first. It does not matter how pretty it looks. It does not matter how good things look. It does not matter how wonderful things seem to be. You have to get to a point where you ask, "Lord, is this what you want me to have? Is this what you want me to do?" You do not want to be saddled with anything that you are not pleased with.

When I was a kid, my mother had a rule: I could not accept candy from strangers. I know that these days, mothers send their children to folk and instruct them to ask for money. "Go tell her it is your birthday," they say. I know that is how we do it these days.

But, when I was growing up many years ago, people had to ask mothers if it was okay to give their children something. Even if they asked properly, I was still taught to say, "No thank you." It did not matter how good the offer was. For example, it was hard for me to turn down chocolate cake. But, even so, I was trained to say, "No thank you. I don't think I want any cake today." I loved chocolate cake and I wanted it so bad. But, it did not matter whether I was hungry or not, I was trained to say, "No thank you."

Invariably, the adult offering the treat understood that I was trained that way. So, eventually they would no longer ask me. They would see me with my mother and ask her if it was all right to give me a piece of candy. Then, my mother would decide because I had to conform to her will. Whatever she said was good for me, is what I was going to have, no matter what I thought about it. Many times I had different ideas about her decision, but what she said went. I was not going to accept candy from anybody until she said it was all right.

Now watch this. The devil can present a pretty package to you, but do not fool yourself. The devil can give you candy. The devil will offer you what looks like fast money. But, do you know what you will do if you are not discerning? You will call it the favor of God. We are very quick to say, "You know God blessed me. That lady left her purse and she never came back. So, I guess that was God trying to bless me. You know the Lord sure works in mysterious ways."

Trust me. You do not want anything that God does not want you to have. You have to submit to His order. Everything that is done for God should be done with a spirit of order. If it is done without a spirit of order, it is not done in the spirit that God would have it to be executed. It is extremely important that you understand this in the context of what God would have us to do.

Let all things be done decently and in order.

\- *I Corinthians 14:40*

God is saying to us that everything in our lives has to line up decently and in order. Everything, not some things, or a few things, but everything must line up decently and in order. It has to be done that way. We have to be very careful how we do things.

A lot of times we do things in a way that is not commensurate with our intent. But this verse tells me that you have to get your intent lined up with how you execute things so that when you execute things to get things done, you are also representing the intent that you have behind it.

When you get to a point where you are doing the right thing the wrong way, you are still wrong. It has to be done the right way for it to really be the right thing. You may have been doing a good thing the wrong way, but a good thing has to be done the right way to become the right thing. All things have to be done decently and in order.

> *For God is not the author of confusion, but of peace, as in all churches of the saints.*
>
> \- *I Corinthians 14:33*

What I like here is that the writer mentions church. Some of us want to do things that are right for us. Or, we only want to do things right in certain situations. We want to come to church and do whatever we want to do. Understand what the church is. Church is not our playground. It is not even our house. The Church is God's house.

Now I know people act differently today. But I was trained not to go into someone's house and act in a way that is unseemly. I was trained that when I walked into a house – even as old as I am today – if I walk into your house, this is what I am going to do. I am going to enter your house and stand at the door. I am not going to move until you give me some direction. Why? Because, it is not my house. It is your house. I am going to stand inside of the door. I am not going to go plop myself on your sofa. I am only going to the sofa after you ask me to please sit here. Or say, "Would you like to have a seat?"

I am not going into your refrigerator. I am not going upstairs to your bedroom. I am not going downstairs to your basement. I am not going to check out anything. I am not going to do anything unless I follow your directions in your house. To do otherwise would cause me to be out of order.

When we come into the house of the Lord, we must seek the order of God. If we do not seek the order of God, we insult the one whose house it is. You are not coming over to my house and do whatever you want to do. You are not coming over to my house and go wherever you want to go. If you do that, you insult me.

You cannot come into my house picking up stuff, using stuff, getting my remote and turning stuff on. Let me turn it on. That is my television and my remote. "Now, what would you like to see? Is there a program you would prefer to watch? Let me see what I can turn on for you. Would you like to see the football game, or a comedy show? Let me turn it on for you." Why? I should do that because you are my guest.

When things are done decently and in order you seek the order of the house. When you seek the order of the house, you submit to the order of the house. Your submission to the order of the house is how you are going to get blessed. You do not get blessed when you violate the order of God's house. You get blessed when you submit to the order of God's house.

God is not the author of confusion. Now, many times what is good for you may be okay, but it may not be good if it is thrown into the big picture of things. Often times, there is a big picture that is bigger than you.

So, when you consider the order of God's house, you cannot just consider what is good for you. You have to consider His order. And, His order first is that you are saved. The son of man has come to seek and save that which is lost. So the order of the house is first of all that people might come into a redemptive relationship with Jesus Christ. And, anything that violates that is out of order.

That is why usually there is somebody in the vestibule saying, "good morning" to you when you enter the

House of God. You might be someone who has been burdened down. You might be someone who is sin sick. You might be somebody who is depressed and frustrated with life.

So, we have to make sure that the atmosphere is conducive for the order of the house, because, every time you step into the House of God, you should get a lift. You should get a boost. There should be a Word that is going to explode in your spirit and help you to leave the church more confident and ready to get up tomorrow morning to try it all over again. This should happen simply because you have submitted to the order of the house.

Everybody that has something to do with the order of the house, everybody who has a role in the order of the house, and everybody who is serving in a capacity that lends itself to the order of the house, has to be in order. Otherwise, there is no order in the house. If there is no order in the house, the people who come in are confused. As the scripture says, *God is not the author of confusion, but of peace.* (1 Corinthians 14:33)

You can take command of your destiny when you understand the order of God. Let all things be done decently and in order.

To review, your inner world creates your outer world. Your thoughts and words create life and energy. Your thoughts and words must be subject to the Will and purpose of God. And everything must be done decently and in order.

> *Let the words of my mouth, and the meditation of my heart, be acceptable in thy sight, O Lord, my strength, and my redeemer.*
>
> \- *Psalms 19:14*

We have talked about the words of our mouths and the mediations of our hearts. We have talked about the words that you say and the thoughts that you have. But, watch this. Both your thoughts and your words are to be acceptable, or amenable, or subject to the acceptance of God, or the Will of God. So when you are thinking and speaking, you want what you think and speak to be acceptable in the eyesight of God.

You do not want to speak idle words and think frivolous thoughts because too often you think thoughts that have nothing to do with your destiny. You sometimes speak words that you think have nothing to do with your destiny. If you would expend the same amount of energy toward your destiny as many of us do toward foolishness, we all would be a lot further ahead.

Have you wasted a lot of time in your life making dumb mistakes? Have you done some things that did not make any sense? Have you wasted time… I mean years? He gave you 24 hours a day and you did not just waste a day. You did not just waste a week, or a month. But there were years that you wasted because your life was not in order. Your thoughts and your words were not synchronized to the acceptability of God. You failed God. You failed yourself.

You cannot blame your circumstances. You cannot even blame the people who did not like you. You may say, "My mother did this and my daddy was not around and my mother was like this…" However, you cannot say that because *you* have thoughts and words. Everything in the universe for *you* begins with, revolves around and is given life and energy by *your* thoughts and words. That is the principle. Do not lose the principle. If you lose the principle, you lose the blessing.

If you really want to be blessed, order puts you in position to be blessed. When you are out of order, you are out of position. When your life is out of order, then your life is out of position. Every one of us has shaky days. The thing is to minimize as many shaky days that you have. And, instead, pull yourself into alignment with the purposes of God so that you are living a life of order. Why? Because God does not normally bless disorder.

He may allow disorder for you for a season in order to take you through what you need to go through. The purpose is so that He can give you that faith test that will get your reliance back on him. But, He does not bless disorder.

He will take you through the test. And, at the end of that test, even though it seemed like it was crazy to you, if you are faithful, you will pass the test. He was just trying to make sure that you were going to hold to His unchanging hand until the storm passed over.

> *See then that ye walk circumspectly, not as fools, but as wise.*
>
> \- *Ephesians 5:15*

I want you to know how important the Will of the Lord is. You cannot accept the "candy" of the world without permission and authorization. Circumspectly means that you walk upright. You walk in a way that will not bring shame to the God that saved you. Walking circumspectly means that it has reference. It has sort of a geometric reference. To walk circumspectly means that you walk perpendicular to the Will of God. You walk in agreement with it. You line up with it. You synchronize your will to it. You connect yourself so that you are walking in a way that is pleasing to God.

Do you want to live circumspectly? Do you want to live so that God can use her anytime and anywhere? See then that you use every resource that you have and every fiber of your being to walk in synchronization with the Will of God - *not as a fool, but as wise.*

We live in a knowledge-based society. Right now, there is a lot being said about a knowledge-based economy, because everything that is going to be employable in the future is going to be based on how much you know and how much knowledge you are going to be able to glean. It is not going to be based on being healthy and strong. It is going to be based on knowledge. Machines are doing what people used to do. The technology is already in place.

I saw on CNN, where there is a brand new robot that walks, prepares coffee, and brings it to you on its own. That used to be somebody's job. So for the people who need jobs, they are going to have to move in the direction of a knowledge-based economy. They are going to have to understand that there are certain kinds of disciplines that they will have to learn. There is certain academic knowledge that they will have to know in order to be employable. They will not be able to rely on manual labor skill sets anymore.

I am saying this to say that, when we walk with God, we walk in knowledge. We walk in wisdom. We live in a world now that is full of knowledge, but not necessarily of wisdom. I know a whole lot of people who are smart, but are stupid. I know a whole lot of people who have degrees behind their names. They have all kinds of attainment. They have all kinds of things that they have accomplished. They are very accomplished people. They are very erudite, inimitable type of folk, but they are not wise. They operate foolishly, because their lives are not in order.

It is important that you not only have knowledge, but that you have wisdom. The Bible says: *"with all of thy getting, get understanding."* (Proverbs 4:7) Get wisdom, because wisdom is the principle thing. Knowledge means nothing if you don't understand what you know.

Redeeming the time, because the days are evil.

- *Ephesians 6:16*

If you are in the order of God, you do not have time to waste time. You have to be about your Father's business. Deliver me from these folk that are just so laid back so much that they are not accomplishing anything. They do not care about anything. No matter what happens it happens and if it does not happen, so what. You have to have some purpose and intent in your life. You have to wisely be a steward over the time that God has given to you.

Life is short. The older you get, the shorter it gets. The older you get the more you start looking around and the people you used to know are not there anymore. The older you get, the more you begin to understand that life is shorter and shorter.

When I was a child it was an eternity for Christmas to come. It seemed as though Christmas never came. It seemed as though my birthday never came. Now every other week it looks like I am having a birthday. Why? Because the more time you have, the shorter time gets. You must redeem the time. You must make good use of your time, not foolishly, but wisely. Stop wasting time.

Stop procrastinating. Time is a precious gift from God. Use it wisely.

CHAPTER 11

The Principle of Balance

"Line Up!"

There is one more principle that I would like to add to the principle of order and that is "balance." Order is balance. When things are lined up properly, they are lined up in a balanced fashion. The weight of one side counteracts the weight of the opposite side.

Take me for example. I used to think I could not laugh because I was a preacher and a pastor. I was young and saved and I did not want people to mistake who I was. I did not want them to discount me.

I had to learn that I could laugh sometimes. I have permission to laugh sometimes, because my life needs balance. I have to deal with so many serious things all the time. I need something to counteract what weighs so heavily on me on the other side. So you have to have balance in your life

. People of faith have to have balance too. Saved folk have to have balance. We all have to laugh for a minute. You feel better sometimes when you laugh. And, that is exactly what God does to our enemies.

> *The wicked plotteth against the just, and gnasheth upon him with his teeth.*
>
> *The Lord shall laugh at him for he seeth that his day is coming.*
>
> \- *Psalms 37:12-13*

When folks come up against you and try to cut you off and when people are trying to kill you and the haters are hating and the viciousness is high, the Bible says the Lord laughs at them because He knows that there day is coming. If God can laugh, you ought to be able to look at some things sometimes – even though you have the weight of the world on your shoulder – and laugh. Sometimes you do not know if you are on top of the world, or the world is on top of you. But either way, you have to be able to have balance.

> *Wherefore be ye not unwise, but understanding what the will of the Lord is.*
>
> \- *Ephesians 5:17*

Do not waste your time being foolish. You need to understand what the Will of the Lord is. You need to put your heart in synchronization with God's Will so that you can gain an understanding of what the Will of the Lord is. Why? Because God's Will is what you want.

If your life is characterized by confusion, conflict frustration, lack of direction, meaning, or insight, it is an indication that most likely your life lacks order.

> *In those days was Hezekiah sick unto death. And Isaiah the prophet the son of Amoz came unto him, and said unto him, Thus saith the Lord, Set thine house in order; for thou shalt die, and not live.*
>
> \- *Isaiah 38:1*

Isaiah comes to Hezekiah and says, "Look man, you might as well go on and get things together. You are sick and your time may not be that long. It is time for you to set your house and your life in order." And what did Hezekiah do?

> *Then Hezekiah turned his face toward the wall, and prayed unto the Lord.*
>
> \- *Isaiah 38:2*

Whenever your back is against the wall, you have to pray yourself out. Have you ever had to pray yourself through some stuff? You talked to folk and that did not work. You cursed them out and they cursed you back. You slit the tires and threw the brick through the window. You did everything that you felt like doing. You wasted a lot of time trying to do something to get back at them.

I will suggest to you that when your life is the way it is and you are up against the wall, pray your way out. Don't ever say, "Well I guess we can't do anything now, but pray." Because you should have been praying before it happened. When you say you have done everything else that means you forgot God. And, when you finished doing what you were going to do, then and only then did you decide to call on His name.

It is much like people who are going to get evicted tomorrow and they come to you like it is an emergency. They come to you when they are already four months behind. It seems like when they got one, or two months behind, it would have been a little easier to help them out. But some people want to wait until it is an emergency. Well, an emergency on your part does not create an emergency on my part.

In his prayer, Hezekiah said,

> *Remember now, O Lord I beseech thee, how I have walked before thee in truth and with a perfect heart, and have done that which is good in thy sight. And Hezekiah wept sore.*
>
> \- *Isaiah 38:3*

You have to live your life so that when you get in the worse part of your life, you can lean on a track record of relationship with God. You had better live so, because that day is coming. The day comes without you understanding that it is coming. The day is going to come when you are at the lowest ebb of your life. The day is going to come when it looks like all hope is gone and there is nothing else on which you can lean.

That is precisely the time when you are going to have to lean on your relationship with God. You are going to have to say, "Lord, I served you when I had a chance. I did what I could. I prayed and I was good to other folk and I did what I needed to do. I know that does not exempt me from trouble. But, I just want you to know that I have a good track record because I kept myself in order."

Hezekiah began to weep and the Word of the Lord came onto Isaiah saying:

> *Go, and say to Hezekiah, Thus saith the Lord, the God of David thy father, I have heard thy prayer, I have seen thy tears; behold, I will add unto thy days fifteen years.*
>
> \- *Isaiah 38:5*

You would be surprised to find out what God will do when you get down to your last – when you get down to your lowest ebb. You would be surprised to find out what God will do when you fall on your knees and beseech him with your whole heart. You would be surprised to learn what He will do for your children when you cannot do anything with them – when all you have is a prayer on your lips and a track record of relationship on your heart.

You would be surprised at what He will do with your financial situation when you are down and out and you do not know how you are going to make it. You do not know where you are going to go. You would be surprised to find out what God will be able to do with you if you open up your heart and give him glory and praise. You should give Him glory and praise for what He has done for you in a tight spot, in a hard spot, in a tough place.

As a matter of fact, some of you who are reading this right now had good times in your life, but you found God when times got tough. You found God when times got tight. You found God when you did not have anything else to do but rely and depend on Him and God gave you another chance.

You did have a relationship with Him, and He gave you another chance. You did walk circumspectly to His Will. You sought to put everything in your life around the circle and the circumference of His Will. And because of that, God had compassion on you and He gave you another chance.

That is why you are still alive. He gave you another chance. That is why you are not out in the cold tonight – another chance. That is why you have not lost your mind – another chance. Thank God for another chance. Praise Him right now for another chance. Thank Him because you got another chance.

You did not even think that you were worthy of another chance. You did not even think that you deserved another chance. But God gave you another chance. That is why you can get up every day with a smile on your face. You can get up every day knowing who you are in Him. You can get up every day having the confidence and the assurance that God is on your side because He did not bring you this far to leave you now.

You are still in His Will. You are walking in it. You are taking command of your destiny, because you have your mind made up. You have your heart in order. No matter what is going on in your life, God will keep you in perfect peace as you keep your mind stayed on Him.

Get yourself in order. God is ready to bless folk that are in order. He is ready to lift up people that dare to be in order. He is ready to bless you tremendously and supernaturally if you are in order.

From this day forward be in order, because it is written:

> *...Eye hath not seen, nor ear heard, neither have entered into the heart of man, the things which God hath prepared for them that love him.*
>
> \- *I Corinthians 2:9*

Do you love Him? Act like you love Him. If you are trying to keep things in order, act like you love Him. Praise Him like you love Him. Dance like you love Him. Open up your mouth like you love Him. Set your house in order because you have two choices: live, or die. I wonder if you have decided that you are going to live a life that is pleasing in His sight. Say to yourself, "I am going to keep myself in order."

Line yourself up with the order of God.

CHAPTER 12

God's Purpose for You

"Divine Order"

You would not be here if you really did not think that there were some things that God has specifically for you. It does not matter what age, or stage of life you are in. When there is life, there is always hope. Where there is life, there is always a chance. Where there is life, God has ordained that something has to follow.

You would not wake up another day if God's purpose for you was already fulfilled. You would have no reason to live another day. God would say, "Okay, time is up." You would not have a reason to live another day unless God has purpose and intent for your life.

Understand that every day that you have is a gift from God. Many times you may wake up in the morning and say, "Okay what is so good about today? It is not a good morning for me." But understand this. In the true context of life, unless God has purpose and intent in your life it just does not happen. Things do not just happen. God has purpose.

God has intent. There is order involved. God has things that need to be released. Your life is a testament to the fact that in this generation God wants to release some things in your life that are important. They are crucial. That is why you cannot waste your life. You cannot abort it. You cannot tear it up. You cannot treat it any kind of way. You cannot live a raggedy life.

You have got to have some scruples about yourself. You have to be concerned about how you present yourself, especially if you are a "King's Kid." You have to be concerned about how you deal with life situations. You have to be concerned about your response. You have to be cognizant of what your reaction is to things, even when people do not treat you the way they should treat you. Why? Because you are an agent and representative for the Kingdom and the King is watching. Are you really representing Him well?

The word represent is really re-present. What it really means is that when you represent, you are re-presenting that which has already been presented to you. So, when you represent, you must re-present. You represent God by re- presenting Him to the world. When people look at you, they should see the representation of God.

They should see you re-presenting God to them from your perspective so that people see God and not some man upstairs. Or, not some face in a cloud. But they should see God presented because you have re-presented God to them. It is important that you understand this as you take command of your destiny and direct your future with the power of God being the source of your supply.

We started out by saying that everything in the universe begins with, revolves around and receives life and energy from our thoughts and words. It is our thoughts and words that are so very crucial in terms of our future destiny. You have to watch what you say and you have to watch what you think.

Think good thoughts. Think on things that are going to get you to that next level in God. Spend your time thinking about things that are going to help you to better represent God in your life. Then, once you think it, use words that are designed to get you to that special place in God.

God wants you to be in a position where those things that you think and say are the creative material that takes you to the next level because your words are things. Scripture states:

> *"...as he thinketh in his heart, so is he..."*
>
> \- *Proverbs 23:7*

So what you are thinking is what you become. What you speak is what you become. You put words in the atmosphere that have to be in sync with the Word of God. When they are in sync with the Word of God, then they produce God's ordained result.

However, if your words and your thoughts violate what God's intent is for your life, then you cancel, negate and decertify the Will of God and the intent of God in your life. If you are going to constantly say to yourself, "He is not going to do it." "God is not going to do it," then He is not going to do it, because it takes faith for you to believe that God will do exactly what He says.

In the last chapter, we talked about order because your thoughts and your words need to flow in divine order. There is an order that God requires in order for you to receive that which your thoughts and your words are creating. We defined it as the regulation of a prevailing course, or arrangement of things that reinforce the intent of God.

Order is God's structure being set up to reinforce His intent. God's intent in your life is reinforced by the order that He presents in your life. You have to say, let the words of my mouth and the meditation of my heart be what God's order is for your life. Acceptable does not just mean that He accepts it. It means that your words and your meditations -- or the thoughts of your heart -- are lining up and are in sync with what God's intent is for your life, so that everything flows in divine order.

Refuse to sit back and passively let life happen. Instead, aggressively and proactively envision and unleash the power of God in your life. I am talking about the power to take command of your own destiny. You cannot do that passively. You cannot just sit back and let people continue to knock you upside the head. You cannot let people continue to tell you things that you know God has not said. They don't have to like you. If they want to, they can hate you. That's okay. Just do not believe what they believe about you.

When you start believing what they believe about you, then you have to adopt their view of who you are. You should not be guided, nor defined, by their view of who you are. You should be guided and defined by God's view of who you are. You have to accept what He says and then cast out those things that are imaginary – things that do not line up with God, or things that other people might think or say. You cannot be so guided by what other folk think of you.

Some of us are so busy trying to please other people that we cannot sleep at night. We take "Tylenol No. 25" and then we have to take "Pepto Bismol" to go with that. Our heads are all upset and our stomachs upset. We can't sleep. We can't do anything, because of what somebody said. You have to get pass what others say. We are all human beings so we listen to what other people say even though what other people say can hurt.

But you have to understand and have the power to rebuke it. It does not have to attach itself to you. It may have stung you, but take the knife out. That is your only chance for survival. If you leave the knife in, you will die. If you take it out, you have a chance to live.

If you want to live, you have to lean to what God says about you. Do not sit back and passively let life happen. Aggressively and proactively envision and unleash the power of God in your life. In order to do that, I am still talking about thoughts, words and order.

I don't want you to think that it's a magic formula. I want you to understand that you have to know who you are in God. In order to be able to command your destiny, you have to know who you are.

You are probably feeling empty right now because you do not quite know. You are not sure. You have to know who you are in God. Once you know who you are in God all the rest becomes easy.

We need to know who we are as the people of God. You cannot call anything down from heaven if you do not know who you are. When you are going through tight spots and really going through hell and high water, you have to get help from heaven. You are not going to get any help from heaven unless you know who you are.

Know ye not that ye are the temple of God, and that the Spirit of God dwelleth in you?

I Corinthians 3:16

Do you know that you are the temple of God? Stop there and marinate on this for a short while. Do you know who you are? Do you know that God has erected you as a temple of God? Do you know that even though your body may have some flaws in it, it is still the temple of God. You may have some issues here and there and there might be a few cracks, but you are the temple of God.

For example, before you can get a certificate of occupancy for a building, you have to do an inspection of the premises. You have a punch list and you have to go through and inspect every crack and crevasse. Even then, you have to understand that as the building settles there are going to be more cracks.

Just like the building, you begin to settle, and as life begins to settle on you, there are more cracks. That does not mean that the building is not strong. It does not mean that the building is not constructed properly. It just means that the longer you settle in one place, the more cracks you are going to have. Even though your body is the temple of God, it has a few cracks.

My body has a few cracks too. We all have a few cracks, but do you know who you are? Do you know that you are the temple of God and that the spirit of God resides, dwells and lives inside of you? Do you know that?

You are not a human being looking for a spiritual experience. You are a spirit being navigating through the human experience. God created you as a spirit being, a place where His spirit dwells on the inside of you. Do you know that you are a temple of God?

As a matter of fact, when we come together to praise God for corporate praise and worship, teaching and preaching and the ministry of the Word, do you know that what is happening is that your temple and my temple are coming together. Our spirits – the spirit God put in you and the spirit God put in me – come together and explode in the worship experience.

I believe that the church building has been dedicated and anointed to the glory of God. But I also believe that the anointed people who enter the church are what make the worship experience alive. In other words, when the

Jesus in me and the Jesus in you get together, difficult people become easy to love.

It gets a little bit easier because of who you are. Do you know who you are? If you do not know, you cannot command anything. You cannot go any further until you know who you are. I have some real stuff to share with you, but you cannot get it – you cannot appropriate it and it will not work for you until you understand who you are.

When Abraham Lincoln signed the Emancipation Proclamation he said

> *Four score and seven years ago, our fathers brought on this continent a new nation conceded in liberty and dedicated to the proposition that all men are created equal and endowed by their creator with certain unalienable rights and upon those rights are life, liberty and the pursuit of happiness.*

He signed the Emancipation Proclamation and freed the slaves … and, the slaves kept picking cotton. Do you know who you are?

"Man hold it! You do not have to do that anymore. You are not a slave any more. Abraham Lincoln signed the Emancipation Proclamation." But, they just kept on picking. When you do not know who you are, you cannot exercise the power that you have. You cannot walk in your destiny until you know who you are. You cannot be who you are until you know who you are. When you know who you are, you start the journey to becoming what you need to be.

Your body is a temple. You are the temple of God and His spirit dwells and lives inside of you. Scripture states:

> *"Know ye not that ye are the temple of God, and that the spirit of God dwelleth within you. If any man defile the temple of God, him shall God destroy for the temple of God is holy, which temple ye are."*
>
> *-1 Corinthians 3:16-17*

You are holy and designed by God.

I had a brother ask me, "Pastor, is it a sin to smoke?" Let me put it to you this way and I showed him this scripture. I said, "Whatever defiles the temple … whatever you do that defiles the integrity of the temple, and is destructive to the temple is in violation of what God has ordained for your life."

> *But ye are a chosen generation, a royal priesthood, an holy nation, a peculiar people; that ye should shew forth the praises of him who hath called you out of darkness into his marvelous light:*
>
> - *I Peter 2:9*

I have to get you to know who you are. I have to share this Word and release some power. We are chosen. I want you to know that if you are the temple of God, God has chosen you. He has chosen you first of all for His spirit to dwell inside of you. Next, He has chosen you so that you have access to power that is going to take you to the next level in your life. You are chosen for this generation. That is why you were not born in the 1700s, or 1800's, or 1900's. You were born when you were born and the year you were born, because God has something for you in this generation through the spirit that He put inside of you that has to be released.

He has you here on purpose for a purpose. Isn't it funny how little children can adapt to computers right away. They are not like us old folks. We have to sit down and read a manual, like *Computers for Dummies 101*. We have to figure out what a program is on a computer and how to operate it.

But little kids are automatically inquisitive. God has programmed and prewired them for this generation. God has already prepared them for what is coming ahead. They are already armed with a computer.

Kids do not say that they are scared of computers. They gravitate toward computers, even if it is just a computer game. Why? Because there is something in the computer that has already been predisposed inside of them that they are going to have to use to access all kinds of things in their generation.

God knows that you have been chosen for such a time as this. So stop discounting yourself. Begin to aggressively and proactively see what God has in your future and take command of it. Take authority and direct responsibility for it because God has chosen you for this particular time. This is a chosen time for you.

We are a royal priesthood, a holy nation, a peculiar people. Everybody is not going to like you. Let me burst your bubble right quick and make a prophetic announcement to you – Everybody is not going to like you. Everybody is not going to like your style, or your tactics. Everybody is not going to like the way you wear your hair, or the way you dress. Everybody is not going to like the way you talk. Why? Because you are peculiar.

That means that you do not appeal to everybody. But you are not worried about appealing to everybody. You are trying to please God.

Pleasing God automatically puts you at variance with other folks sometimes. Other folks cannot understand a God pleaser. Other people do not understand that because they are doing their own thing their own way that is what their life is all about. But I am here to tell you that when you please God, something spectacular begins to happen in your life because there is an at oneness with him that you begin to feel and sense in your spirit. Other people do not always understand that. They are looking at you funny and saying, "He is strange. She is strange. He is peculiar." But I am telling you that people who are chosen by God often look and act peculiar.

It is peculiar to love folk that hate you. That is not normal at all. It is peculiar to do good to them that hate you, or to pray for them that despitefully use you. That is peculiar stuff. That is not the way the world rolls. That is not the way they do it in the streets.

You have to get to a point where you understand that following your destiny sometimes means that you are misunderstood. People do not know why you are praying about everything and why you are not worried about anything because you are giving it to God.

Promise me that you will have a peace that surpasses all understanding. Keep your heart and your mind together while everything around you is crumbling. How is it that many of you have not lost your mind in the middle of everything that you have been through and are yet going through?

You are walking by faith and not by sight. There is a destiny before you and a spirit of God in you. You are the temple of God. You are able to take a licking and keep on ticking because you know you have stuff in you that the world does not understand. God's Word will always back you up.

I am telling you that when you access and command your destiny, God will back you up. First, you have your thoughts and your words in line with him and you are in order. When you do that, it is time for you to take command of your destiny and God's Word will back you up.

CHAPTER 13

God's Thoughts Are Above Our Thoughts

"Command Your Day!"

For my thoughts are not your thoughts, neither are your ways my ways, saith the Lord.

- *Isaiah 55:8*

I am so glad that God's thoughts are not our thoughts, because sometimes some of our thoughts are not good. Have you ever really wanted to hurt somebody? I mean you thought about it. Have you ever had an idea in your mind of how you were going to get somebody back? You had to rebuke that thought so quick because you knew that was going to get you in a whole lot of trouble, even though it sounded like a good idea at the time.

What I am so glad about is that God's thoughts are so far above ours. His ways are so much higher than ours. That is why we love God because we serve a God that is smarter than we are. We serve a God who has an idea of us that is better than the idea that we have of ourselves. His thoughts are above ours. No matter what we think ourselves to be, His thoughts are above that and we have to go through the process of getting our thoughts in line with His.

We have to lift our thoughts because when we lift our thoughts, we lift our thoughts in the area where God is. God is never scraping the bottom of the barrel. God is always the cream that is on the top. His ways and His thoughts are always above ours.

Dare to dream big. Stop dreaming so small. If you are dreaming within the parameters and capacity of your ability to produce, then you are dreaming too small. But if you are dreaming in an area and in a realm that demands supernatural intervention, then you have given in to God's neighborhood

I think the problem is that too many of us dream too small. We think too small. We expect too little even though we serve a big God. We should expect big things from Him. Do not listen to the little things people have to say about what to expect. Expect big things from a God who we know is bigger, better, smarter, wiser and more resourceful – a God whose ways are above our ways and thoughts above our thoughts.

Tell other people who do not understand you that they do not know the God you serve. The God you serve is thinking at a level that you and I are not able to think on. The God we serve is thinking on a much higher level. He has His own ways. He has His own unique actions, and, He has supernatural abilities. He has capacity that is beyond our capacity to even think of His capacity. So you need to understand that what God has in store for you evidently is out of this world, because it has to be something higher than what we are thinking. That is why Paul said in Corinthians:

> *…eye hath not seen, nor ear heard, neither have entered into the heart of man, the things which God hath prepared for them that love him.*
>
> \- *I Corinthians 2:9*

So what are you going to do… talk down what is in store for you? Are you going to begin to deny what you have in the lay-away?

Maybe you cannot get it out. Maybe you do not have enough money to get it out of the lay away, but you have your receipt. And, your receipt has your name on it. It means that one day you are going to go up to the counter to get what God has in store for you.

His thoughts are higher and His ways are higher. You cannot see your way out, but God has a way that is so much higher than your way. No wonder you cannot see it. God said I do not want you to see it; I want you to believe it. If you can believe that I will get you out, then I will show you how high my ways are. If you can trust me, when you cannot face me, I will show you great and mighty things that you know not.

> *For as the heavens are higher than the earth, so are my ways higher than your ways, and my thoughts than your thoughts.*
>
> \- *Isaiah 55:9*

First of all, God is thinking about you. His thoughts are higher about you than you have of yourself. Many times people use conceit as a defense mechanism. They have these high ideas of themselves that are lofty and based on conceit and big headedness. God says you would not even have to put out all of that noise – which is sometimes out of insecurity, because we want people to stay away from us. Sometimes we are too insecure about what other people might see if they get too close. So we do a lot of bragging and a lot of this and the other about ourselves. Some of us are a little too happy with ourselves.

But then God says that there is a realm that you have never touched, but he already has you in mind. You are already in it, even though you have never seen, or touched it. And, in order that you might obtain access to it, He says, "I need you to believe me for it."

That is why there are some new millionaires reading this book. Not everybody. Just those who believe that God has a realm in which he is thinking of you, and that it is much higher than what you and other folks think of you.

God has something bigger for you than you even have for yourself. He has a bigger thought. He has something in mind that you know nothing about. It is something that you have not even accessed yet. There are doors that are open that you do not even know exist.

You are asking God for stuff that you can see. You are saying, "Lord if you can just get me through that door. If you can just get me pass that. If you can just do this. If you can just do that."

God says, "Shut up!" He has some doors that have not even been constructed yet. He has stuff that you do not even know about yet. He has some stuff for you to walk through that you did not even know existed. He has some people to connect you to that you are not even going to understand how you got connected to them. You are going to look up and all you will know is that you already know them. You will have their phone number. You will have their email. They will tell you to call them, and just like that, you are one call away from where you need to be in God.

You are one relationship. You are one power lunch. You are one email away. You are one contact. You are one introduction away. Somebody is going to introduce you to somebody who you did not even know was anybody. But you are going to find out that it was just the person you needed to know when God gets finished with it.

> *For as the rain cometh down, and the snow from heaven, and returneth not thither, but watereth the earth, and maketh it bring forth and bud, that it may give seed to the sower, and bread to the eater:*

> *So shall my word be that goeth forth out of my mouth: it shall not return unto me void, but it shall accomplish that which I please, and it shall prosper in the thing whereto I sent it.*
>
> *Isaiah 55:10-11*

For as the rain cometh down and the snow from heaven and returneth not thither. Rain does not go back up God sends the rain down. In fact, do you know what rain is? Rain is condensation of atmospheric vapor that is caused by conflicting behavior in the heavens. Rain comes down because a high pressure system collides with a low pressure system.

Some of you are in a rainy season in your life, because you have highs and you have lows. You have good things happening and bad things happening. While everything seems to be wonderful, everything is awful at the same time.

In other words, there has been a collision between your high pressure and your low pressure. And, the collision is causing a rain storm. The rain descends, the Bible says. The snow comes down from heaven, the Bible says. And, it comes down with intent and purpose, which means that every high system and every low system that had to collide did it on purpose. That is the only way God can send rain to the earth.

Rain to the earth is the only way that the trees, flowers, crops and food can grow. The seed has to come to the soil for bread to come to the eater. The rain comes down to bring forth bud and to give seed to the sower. That is why the rain comes and it gives bread to the eater.

At my house, I have a plant that came from my mother's home-going celebration. The plant is just a little reminder. I have it sitting in somewhat of a strange place. But that is all right because it reminds me of my mother. The plant cannot talk, but it has a way of letting me know that it needs rain. It needs water. It has a way of getting real droopy on me when the leaves go down. And, the plant bows almost as if it is in prayer.

I do not have a green thumb and I do not know anything about taking care of plants. I could not grow anything if you gave me the seeds, the sun and the water. I could not grow it.

But, I learned something about plants though. I learned that at the time when the plant is the most droopy, that is the time when all it needs is some sustenance and water. I do not have time to love on a plant. I am not Martha Stewart. I do not know anything about all that. But when the plant is droopy, I go to the hydrant, get a pitcher of water and pour it into the plant. Then I go on about my business. Then pretty soon, the plant is no longer droopy.

You see, the rain in your life is designed to minister to you when you are droopy. You had better start thanking God for rain in your life. There has to be rain to appreciate the sunshine. There has to be some storm and you need to thank God for it, because the storm is producing something that has a far more exceeding weight of glory in your life. It is helping you – with your droopy self – to come back alive.

God has been doing this and you have been praying and trusting and believing God even when you were droopy. Then God came by and let the rain fall on you. And, when the rain fell, you started getting strength.

> *Even the youth shall faint and be weary, and the young men shall utterly fall:*
>
> *But they that wait upon the Lord shall renew their strength; they shall mount up with wings as*

> *eagles; they shall run, and not be weary; and they shall walk, and not faint.*
>
> \- *Isaiah 40:30-31*

The rain has to fall. Your high pressure and your low pressure have to collide every now and then. Claps of thunder need to take place and lightning will strike.

> *So shall my word be that goeth forth out of my mouth; it shall not return unto me void, but it shall accomplish that which I please, and it shall prosper in the thing whereto I sent it.*
>
> \- *Isaiah 55:11*

The Word is going to back you up. The Word that goes out of my mouth – God says – is going to back you up. It is just like the rain that falls that has purpose and intent to save you from being droopy. The Word that goes forth out of His mouth shall not return void. Whatever God has said and whatever His Word is over you in your life, has got to come to pass because it cannot go back up. Rain does not go up, it comes down. It has purpose and intent. It must complete its purpose and intent because God has sent it to do its work. He said I am going to send my Word and it is going to back you up.

Do you believe that?

> *...but it shall accomplish that which I please and it shall prosper in the thing whereto I sent it.*
>
> - *Isaiah 55:11*

God says, "It will accomplish what I please." He is going to measure your rain because He is going to make sure that the amount of rain He sends is enough to accomplish what needs to be watered. He wants to make sure that it is enough to resuscitate what is droopy.

Sometimes you say, "Lord why has my time been so long? It looks like everyone else has gotten through and they have gone on with their lives and here I am." You need it to rain. Your ground is parched and dry. God needs to send more rain there. But, He is not going to allow it to return void. So, whatever is happening is measured.

God will not put more on you than you can bear. The scripture says it this way:

> *There hath no temptation taken you but such as is common to man: but God is faithful, who will not suffer you to be tempted above that ye are able; but will with the temptation also make a way to escape, that ye may be able to bear it.*
>
> - *1 Corinthians 10:13*

But God will — with the temptation test and trial – give you a way of escape by which you might be able to bear it.

He does not always take stuff away from you. But sometimes what He does is allow you to go through it so that you can live above it, while you are yet going through it. Then, you begin to understand how great and how wonderful God really is.

CHAPTER 14

Command Your Destiny

Take Control of Your Life

What does the word command mean? It means to instruct, to dictate, to order, to master, to conquer, to direct with specific authority. Power never concedes anything without a demand. You cannot turn the lights on in a building without flipping a switch. There is a switch that turns the lights on and that switch is the demand for electricity from the generator to power the lights. The demand is there – the switch is turned on which signifies the demand that releases the power.

When you get in your car and you have a key, a key represents a demand. When placed properly into the ignition, a key is the essential element that transmits an electronic signal to the motor, which triggers the demand for the power. Power never concedes anything without a demand

. Nothing ever leaves heaven until a request for it is sent up from the earth. God is waiting to hear what you have to say. God is waiting for you.

> *"Oh, what peace we often forfeit.*
> *Oh what needless pain we bear.*
> *All because we do not carry*
> *Everything to God in prayer."*

Paul said let all of your requests be made known unto God, because heaven cannot release anything until Earth makes a request. Power never concedes anything without a demand.

You have to learn how to command your day. You have to arise in the morning and begin to say that you command this day to fall in line with the purpose and the intent of God no matter who from hell is assigned to try to come against and subvert the natural order that God has for your day

You will stand in victory ultimately if you command your day. Do not look at stuff and say, "Que sera sera –

whatever will be will be." "Well, that is the way folks are." "Well, you know that is how it is." "Well, it is what it is." "Well, that is the way the cookie crumbles." No, that is not the way to live your life.

> *I am crucified with Christ; nevertheless I live; yet not I, but Christ liveth in me; and the life which I now live in the flesh I live by the faith of the Son of God, who loved me, and gave himself to me.*
>
> \- *Galatians 2:20*

I wonder if you are living a different life. Do not be ashamed of the life that you are living. You have to get up in the morning and declare that your season of frustration and failure is over. Then, you will be able to walk in a season of success and prosperity, because old things are passed away and behold all things have become new. That is what you have to do. Get up and command each and every day.

Some of you cannot wait until this season is over. As you look at your circumstances, you realize that it has been a season of transition, elevation and completion. And, you wonder what it is that you are taking into your next season.

You are entering a new season. This is a new beginning for you. As God allows you to go on to your next season, it is not by accident. Because if he did not have a purpose and intent for your life – a way higher than what you are, or a thought higher than what you are – he would take you before your next season comes.

But, I am here to declare that your season of frustration and failure is over. God is erasing the slate for you. This is a season of new beginnings for you. You have a new beginning coming. Do not let anyone count you out. The game is not won at half time. You win the game when the time runs out. Your time has not run out yet. God evidently has you here for a purpose. You still have time.

Tell yourself that you still have time. You may have wasted some time, but you still have time. You may have done wrong, but you still have time. You may have made mistakes, but you still have time.

> *And the same day, when the even was come, he saith unto them, Let us pass over unto the other side.*

> *And when they had sent away the multitude, they took him even as he was in the ship. And there were also with him other little ships.*
>
> \- *Mark 4:35-36*

Some of you think that you are the only one going through hard times. You think that nobody is going through what you are going through. There are other ships in the same sea that you are in. There are other folk who are going through stuff. And, I promise you that there are people in the same sea going through stuff worse than you.

I know that what they are going through is worse than you, because they do not have Jesus on board. At least you have Jesus on board the ship with you. The Bible says that they took Him even as He was in the ship. And, there were with Him also other little ships.

> *And there arose a great storm of wind, and the waves beat unto the ship, so that it was now full.*
>
> \- *Mark 4:37*

Well it was a wonder that they had not capsized and drowned. The boat was full of water. How in the world are you surviving?

You have been in a big storm, big waves, big water and your boat is full. Have you just had enough and cannot take anymore, because your boat is full? Is your boat full? If your boat is full, that should mean that you are drowning. It means that your boat is sinking. But somehow, even though your boat is full, it is still sailing and not sinking.

And, do you know why it is sailing and not sinking? Because Jesus is on board the ship. You do not know why it is that you have not gone under yet. You do not understand why your business is still floating. You do not understand why your family is still floating. You do not understand why you still have a roof over your head. You do not understand why they still have not come to get your car out of the driveway. You do not understand how half your stuff is in the pawn shop. You do not understand what is going on. But somehow, instead of sinking, God has you still sailing with a full boat. It does not make sense, but it is because Jesus is on board.

> *And he was in the hinder part of the ship, asleep on a pillow; and they awake him, and say unto him, Master, carest thou not that we perish?*
>
> \- *Mark 4:38*

That is even more ridiculous. How can you go to the hull of the ship? How can you go down in a ship that was already full of water and find Jesus still asleep on a pillow. God moves in mysterious ways.

They woke him up:

> *Master, carest thou not that we perish?*
>
> *And, he arose and he rebuked the wind, and said unto the sea, Peace be still. And the wind ceased, and there was a great calm.*
>
> \- *Mark 4:38-39*

Remember, rain is a collision of high pressure and low pressure systems that causes a convulsion of wind that sends rain out of the clouds. God does not bring the clouds, but the wind brings the condensation of atmospheric vapor called rain out of the clouds.

When you see rain here, He does not deal with the rain, because the rain is a consequence of the two atmospheres colliding. Jesus always gets to the root cause of your problem. He does not necessarily fool around with the symptoms. He did not say he was rebuking the rain. They were in a storm. He did not rebuke the rain. He rebuked the wind.

When he rebuked the wind, the sea got calm. When he rebuked the wind, the rain stopped. God has a way of getting to the nitty gritty of your situation and turning your situation upside down even though it looks ridiculous and you ought to be sinking, but you are sailing. Somehow, or another, God fixes that thing so that even though you think that you are sinking, you are really sailing to a place where God can bring everything under calm subjection.

God is about to bring some calmness to your life. All that uneasiness and unevenness is about to dissipate in your life. Those symptoms that have been colliding with one another are now going to stop fighting. You are going to see God do this and you are going to see a calm shift. You are going to be moving in a calm direction.

There is going to be a calm. It might still be storming, but you are going to have a sense of calm that you never thought you could have in the middle of a storm. I am not telling you that the water is going to stop. I am telling you that the wind is going to stop blowing to a point where you can go calmly into your future and command your destiny.

Here is what He did. He said, "Wind, peace," - there is a comma after peace. You know how we used to sing

Peace Be Still. No, you have to stop. The comma says pause. He says, He rebukes the winds' boisterousness. He speaks to the wind with something completely contrary to what the wind is doing and says peace. I decree that you have the power inside of you to begin to call things that be not as though they were. You have the power to look at situations and circumstances inside of your life -- and I do not care how crazy they are -- to declare and decree peace in that situation.

Declare peace in that family situation, that situation with your children, that job situation, in your internal unrest with yourself. I pray that you understand that your body is the temple of God and that the Holy Spirit resides inside of that temple. You have the power to take command and to direct with specific authority that which God has already designed for your life.

He says to the wind, be calm and the Bible says,

> *And they feared exceedingly, and said one to another, what manner of man is this, that even the wind and the sea obey him.*
>
> \- *Mark 4:41*

I declare unto you that you have the power inside of you to begin to command your destiny so that winds and waves that have been contrary have to calm down. I declare a "calm down" in your life. There are some things in your life that are about to calm down. You do not have to be under some of the pressure that you have been under. Some of the stuff that you thought was just too much for you, God is going to find a way of escape and elimination for you. You are going to begin to feel some relief from that pressure.

It might mean that you have to give up something. It might mean that you have to make some tough decisions. It may mean that you have to part with some things. But I am here to declare that God has an easier, calmer way for you. You are about to receive some calmness in your life.

If you need some calmness in your life, just start thanking God for calmness. Thank Him for His grace and thank Him for His mercy. I stand in agreement with your purposes and your intent. Command your day. Command your year.

Even though the devil tried to knock you down ten, twenty, thirty, forty times, you are still standing. You are not standing still, but, you are still becoming what God would have you to be. The future is bright because you will take command of your destiny and your purpose. Do not allow the devil to come in and destroy you, *"...because greater is He that is in you than He that is in the world."* (1 John 4:4)

Begin to rejoice and say, "Lord, I thank you." Thank Him for the power to command your own destiny. Thank Him for the power to be able to direct your own day, your own year. Know that you can, because God put it inside of you. *You can do all things through Christ which strengthens you.* (Philippians 4:13)

Do you know that He is strengthening you? He is strengthening you in the middle of your situation with your high pressure system and your low pressure system. He is strengthening you even though the rain and the storm have always been around you. God is doing a new thing in your life.

He is opening up a door. He is making a way where there is no way. He is doing a new thing, a mighty thing and a wonderful thing in your life. This is your season of a new beginning and another chance. He would not let you live unless he was in the business of giving you another chance.

Command your destiny. Fulfill your purpose. Live life abundantly, to the full, until it overflows.